OREGON/The Coast

Randy Morse & Keith McDougall

REIDMORE BOOKS OREGON INC.

ISBN 0 - 939284 - 00 - 6
Library of Congress Catalog Number 81 - 50170

overleaf

A rainbow strikes home just south of Cape Kiwanda

For Garfield and Charlotte
R.M.

For my mother
K.M.

Forest scene, Oswald West State Park

We landed at the bottom of a small bay, where we formed a sort of encampment. The spring, usually so tardy in this latitude, was already far advanced. The foliage was budding, and the earth was clothing itself with verdure; the weather was superb, and all nature smiled. We imagined ourselves in the Garden of Eden; the wild forests seemed to us delightful groves, and the leaves transformed to brilliant flowers.

Gabriel Franchere, *Narrative of a Voyage to the Northwest Coast of America,* on arrival at what was to become the site of Fort Astoria, in 1811

Resilience. Near Pacific City

Foreword

Two physical facts shaped my boyhood in Oregon's Willamette Valley more than school, church or parents: the volcanoes of the Cascade Range to the east, and the Coast to the west. No matter how tedious life at times could become, one look out the window was enough to remind me that, not far away, the World — and adventure — were impatiently waiting.

I no longer live in Oregon. In common with most emigrants, I find that the longer I stay away, the more sharply I recall — and miss —what I imagine that I have left behind. I find increasingly that my mental geography of the state is changing, distorting, focusing. Eastern Oregon has become an awkward bulge, containing Smith Rocks, a bit of Bend and Burns, and the Prairie City-Strawberry Mountain area, where I used to tag along with my father, grandfather and assorted uncles on magical (and usually unsuccessful) deer and elk hunting expeditions. The Willamette Valley has become an alarmingly crowded and narrow strip, with the city-states of Portland, Salem and Eugene connected by a ribbon of fast-deteriorating concrete lined with the usual artifacts of North American life in the fast lane.

The Coast now occupies most of my mental map.

I remember driving along Route F in a packed Chevrolet hard-top convertible, straining to beat my brother, sister and cousins to be the first to spot the haze that always hangs over the surf at a distance. I remember saltwater taffy pulling at my fillings, and digging half-heartedly for clams. I remember wearing a State Fair felt hat with a feather stuck in its band, posing seriously with my brother and sister in front of Fort Clatsop, wondering if I looked more like Lewis than Clark.

I remember small houses huddled closely to one another, their gray sides sandblasted, the old cars in their driveways more rust than steel. I remember catching 130 perch and blue-gill inside half-an-hour with Jim Bronson at Siltcoos Lake near Florence.

I remember rolling down the dunes near Honeyman Park wrapped in a plastic sheet. I remember sand in my bologna and pickle sandwich sitting in a steamy car watching the sea pound through and up Devil's Punchbowl. I remember sand in my pant cuffs. Sand in my ears. Sand between my toes, still there after a bath.

Most of all though, I remember the ocean. The incredible fascination of the meeting of sea and surf. The rythmic wave patterns, the intricacy of the lava-lined tidal pools, the relentless tearing and clawing at the continent. Sitting with my back against a huge chunk of warm driftwood, partially protected from the constant wind, looking west, soaking it all in.

Much has been said about the Oregon coast. It is one of the most photographed pieces of shoreline in the world. Oregon/The Coast hopefully does more than simply say and show it all again. Keith McDougall and I have attempted to create an extremely personal book. A book that without being self-indulgent evokes some sense of what the coast of Oregon means to us. A book that we hope will strike some responsive chords in Oregonian and visitor alike.

We have chosen to emphazise sea, sand, rocks, trees, birds and plants in this book. But we have also attempted, through Keith's photographs, to demonstrate that there exists along this shoreline a constant process of synthesis, a melding together of Nature and Man. For us, weathered wood, old boats, rotting rope, rusting car bodies — these are as much a part of the coastal environment as the sea stacks and tidal pools. There will be those who will take exception to this approach. In our defense I can only say that the reader should be aware that this is a subjective look at an immensely varied shoreline. What we have included in this book means something to us. We hope it will to you too.

It is very difficult to produce a proper text for this sort of volume. Most people have the good sense not to even bother with words that usually neither enhance the reader's appreciation of the all-important photographs, nor impart any knowledge that couldn't be picked up just as easily from a tourist brochure. So, what you will find in these pages are quotes. Most of them historical. Some of them literary. Most of them by Oregonians and/or about the Oregon coast. I think that you will find the resultant mix of words and pictures a bit different from the sort of coffee table book you are familiar with.

Take the time to have a look and see for yourself.

If what you see and read brings you even a small measure of the excitement and pleasure that Keith and I experienced in putting Oregon/The Coast together, I'm certain you'll find the time you take, time well spent.

Randy Morse
Eugene, Spring, 1981

Fogarty Creek

We would like to thank:

Marianne, Ulrika and Andreas Morse; John Wood; Noel Stuart; Bob Johnson; John Whaley; Terry McHugh; Ernest Schermann; Alice Hjort; Sue and Merle Williamson; Steve and Pat Morse; Karen McCulloch, Margie McDougall; The Lane County Museum for the photo of the bathers at Nye Beach used on the book's endsheets; The University of Oregon Library for the photo taken near Fogarty Creek which appears on page twelve; all the production people at Stuart Brandle, the color separators and the binders who worked so hard to make Oregon/The Coast a very special book.

R.M. & K.M.

Here I go, singin' low,
Singin' high, bound to fly
To my home.

Come with me, to the sea,
It's a lovely place for you and me to be.

Wish I could learn to take it slow.
Life's so sweet, when I let it flow.

From Cat Mother's "Ode to Oregon," Ray Michaels (Cat Mother Music Inc. — Sealark —B.M.I. — EmmJay Music)

Looking south from Cape Meares

Tow truck, '63 plates, patiently awaiting its next assignment near Gold Beach

The southernmost hundred miles of Oregon's Pacific edge are unusually rural, for only a few unpaved logging roads link it with the interior. Locals perpetuate isolation by refusing to vote funds for highways.

Mark Miller

No milk-toast park denizen this: a large Beechy ground squirrel, near the beach

Detail, cedar driftwood

Tidal hollow, Hug Point

Small tidal crack in rocks below Heceta Head

Approaching evening clouds seen through the branches of a twisted driftwood snag, Cape Meares

The Indians of this reserve represented all that are now
left of the following tribes:

Rogue Rivers	Nestuccas	Euchres
Shastas	Siuselaws	Joshuas
Klamaths	Umtquas	Salmon Rivers
Galeese	Macanotanas	Alceas
Shasta-Costas	Multenotanas	Tillamooks
Coquelles	Chitcoes	Coos
Tootootenas		

Wallis Nash on the population of the Siletz Reserve in 1877. According to him, there were no more than one thousand people living on the Reserve at that time. One thousand people. Nineteen tribes.

Battle Rock, scene of a much-storied struggle between a group of treasure-seekers from Portland and warriors from the Umpqua, Rogue and Coquille bands

This section of Oregon, at that time, contained about two thousand Indian warriors, in the various tribes, who soon became aware that the whites had settled their country, and they soon determined to murder the little band at Port Orford. The latter became alarmed, and determined to retire from their weak fort on the main land, to the rock . . . where they could better fortify themselves against attack. This they accomplished by throwing some old poles across the chasm from the beach to the rock. This rock was a natural fortress —presenting three precipitous sides to the ocean, and being accessible from the land only at one narrow point and there only by the aid of an artificial bridge. The little party of nine men now carried their little brass cannon — a six pounder — and all their guns, pistols and ammunition, on to this rock, and fortified their footbridge or pass-way. This was, for the distance of fifty yards, not more than five feet in width, and if the foot of any person walking upon it slipped, he would fall fifty feet headlong into the sea. At a point sixty yards from the beach, the whites prepared their fortification, leaving a port hole for their cannon. They then loaded the piece with slugs, stones, and bits of iron, to the very muzzle, and prepared themselves for either death or victory — determined, however, to fight to the last extremity. They were not long left in suspense. Their precautions were well timed, for on the following day the tribes of the Umpqua, Rogue and Coquille rivers assembled mustering a thousand or twelve hundred warriors, armed with bows, arrows, and war clubs; they were entirely unacquainted with the use of the death dealing rifle or gunpowder.

They commenced the attack by pouring up the narrow pass-way as thick as they could crowd, with frightful yells; and the little band began to look upon their fate as being already sealed. The whites had chosen a Tennessean, of Jackson nerve, as their commander, who restrained his men until the Indians had approached within ten paces of the mouth of the cannon. Arrows were flying thick and fast against the barricade and over their heads, and the savages were rushing on with exulting yells, as if certain of success. At length the commander, in a loud, firm voice gave the word — "Fire" — and the cannon and rifles simultaneously discharged their messengers of death with a deafening roar. The scene that ensued was one of horror that baffles all description. The yells of confident triumph were changed to shrieks of horror and despair — scores dropped in their tracks, dead — others, wounded, went rolling and tumbling over the sides of the rocky precipice — while hundreds who were unhurt by the discharge,were so frightened that they sprang headlong over the precipice, striking against the craggy rocks in their descent, tumbling from rock to rock, until they struck the roaring and foaming surf, to rise no more. The number of warriors slain at this single discharge was never correctly ascertained, but it was afterward admitted by the Indians that three-fourths of their braves were swept off. The survivors, alarmed beyond measure at the report of the cannon —never having heard the like before, as thunder is unknown in Oregon — fled in consternation to the mountains.

Our little band came off unharmed, but as they had not sufficient powder left for another round, and as they feared a renewal of the attack, when the Indians should have overcome their temporary fright, they concluded to abandon the place. Accordingly, after nightfall, about eleven o'clock, they crawled from their "Rock of Safety," and made their way to the nearest mountain. The mountains being covered with heavy timber and thick undergrowth afforded them secure refuge from their enemies. For nineteen days they wandered over the mountains, bearing a general course toward the Willamette Valley, where they arrived at the end of that time, in safety, subsisting on the way, upon such food as they could procure in the woods.

From that day to this, the scene of their terrible fight has borne the name of the "BATTLE ROCK."

A.N. Armstrong, Oregon, 1857

Detail, ferns against fence

Sleeping sea lions, with another in the water, looking more mineral than animal

The world below the brine,
Forests at the bottom of the sea, the branches and leaves,

Sea-lettuce, vast lichens, strange flowers and seeds, the thick tangle,
openings, and pink turf,

Different colors, pale gray and green, purple, white, and gold, the
play of light through the water,

Dumb swimmers there among the rocks, coral, gluten, grass, rushes,
and the ailment of the swimmers,

Sluggish existences grazing their suspended, or slowly crawling
close to the bottom,

The sperm-whale at the surface blowing air and spray, or disporting
with his flukes,

The leaden-eyed shark, the walrus, the turtle, the hairy
sea-leopard, and the sting-ray,

Passions there, wars, pursuits, tribes, sight in those ocean-depths,
breathing that thick-breathing air, as so many mammals,

The change thence to the sight here, and to the subtle air breathed by
beings like us who walk this sphere,

The change onward from ours to that of beings who walk
other spheres.

Walt Whitman, "The World Beneath the Brine"

Crashing surf at Devil's Churn

Detail, pebbles on beach

Near Cape Lookout

Oh, I have heard her talk about their old home country so many times . . . She would sit and talk to herself about it. She was getting old and that was all she had on her mind.

Mamie Strong, speaking of her great-grandmother, a Coast Native.

Detail, fern leaf

Hidden cave and waterfall, Hug Point

Of all inorganic substances, acting in their own proper nature, and without assistance or combination, water is the most wonderful. If we think of it as the source of all the changefulness and beauty which we have seen in clouds; then as the instrument by which the earth we have contemplated was modelled into symmetry, and its crags chiselled into grace; than as, in the form of snow, it robes the mountains it has made with that transcendant light which we could not have conceived if we had not seen; then as it exists in the form of the torrent, in the iris which spawns it, in the morning mist which rises from it, in the deep crystalline pools which mirror its hanging shore, in the broad lake and glancing river; finally, in that which is to all human minds the best emblem of unwearied unconquerable power, the wild, various, fantastic, tameless unity of the sea; what shall we compare to this mighty, this universal element, for glory and for beauty? Or how shall we follow its eternal changefulness of feeling? It is like trying to paint a soul.

John Ruskin on painting the sea, from "Of Truth of Water"

Hot dog stand, Seaside

If ever God created a paradise here on earth for the red man, it certainly was this locality. Truly for the Indians it was a Paradise lost and for the white man a Paradise gained.

Gwenedde Maple, on Coos County

Millman, planerman, tallyman, loader
Took care of the lumber they knew they oughter
Time was the hauling was done by horses
Good ones and bad ones like some of the bosses

Doesn't seem right, these things should be
No jobs now for you and me
But the sun still sets and up comes the dawn
It is the way of the World — time marches on.

Paul Morgan, lamenting the closure of the lumber mill at Garibaldi,
near Tillamook Bay

A late Spring evening, the light at Cape Lookout visible in the distance, the odd flash from Oceanside in the foreground

The seas and the land slip into the vast blue of evening.
The rolling waves on the shore
crawl in the shadow,
fumbling for the last ray of light on the land,
and vainly return
to the dark sea.
The light
is burning faintly,
fringing the silhouette of a headland
as a quiet stream of golden green.
Again, the light
is blooming a splendor of rose
on the clouds around the zenith,
and holding
a moment of fragile solemnity . . .

Toshihiko Katayama, "Evening Sea"

Fishing boat, Newport

A man who'd go to sea for fun'd go to hell for a pastime.

Malcolm Lowry, from *Ultramarine*

Looking like a major log-jam, straw-sized lily reeds float in a pond on the southern coast

*At noon we weighed and came to sail with a very moderte breeze
which died away to a purfect calm and the flud tide still setting
strong swept us on a reef of rocks, the water was smooth as glass and
the tide still flowing the vessel could receive no material Damage we
run out our Kedge with a small worp and hauled off, the sea breze
cuming in prevented our getting out we veared a scope and moared
with two bowers.*

From the somewhat unschooled pen of First Mate Haswell, writing in the log of the good
ship *Lady Washington* on first entering Tillamook Bay, August 14, 1788.

The subject of our discussion is the Ocean, which was described in olden times as immense, infinite, the father of created things, and bounded only by the heavens; the Ocean, whose never-failing waters feed not only upon the springs and rivers and seas, according to the ancient belief, but upon the clouds, also, and in certain measure upon the stars themselves; in fine, that Ocean which encompasses the terrestrial home of mankind with the ebb and flow of its tides, and which cannot be held nor enclosed, being itself the possessor rather than the possessed.

Hugo Grotius, *Mare Liberum,* 1609

Surf at sunset seen from Seal Rock

A coastal resident, doing what most of his fellows do at the first sign of an itchy nose

The Cycle; a dead leaf rests, nurturingly, on a living fern

Morning mist creeps into lush crevices north of Sister Rocks, southern coast

The weather was moderate the year around; the mountains, hills and valleys were literally alive with deer, elk, bear, panther, wildcats, California lions, and lynx, and there were even some wolves and coyotes. There were rabbits, mink, beaver, otter and squirrels in great abundance. In the fall and winter the air was almost darkened with ducks and geese, to say nothing of the quail, grouse and partridge to be found at other times. The streams and bay contained all kinds of fish, as well as clams, crabs, mussels and other shell fish. Many kinds of berries in season covered the divides of various valleys . . .

Gwenedde Maple, on Coos County

Window, Yaquina Head Lighthouse

Standing, while not as spectacularly, equally as aloof and just as independently as the Light its resident operates, the Heceta Head keeper's house, illuminated by the low sun of early evening

The old man doffed his clothes, and squeezed himself, head first, through the hole. Soon a light appeared through another smaller hole on the other side. This light came from a heap of brushwood thrown together on a kind of shelf at one side of the underground cavity about eight feet square by six feet high in the middle.

The old Indian, having set fire to the brushwood, lay down by the side of it on the shelf, and began crooning over a most mournful ditty, he lying with his face downwards on his crossed arms.

The smoke drifted out through the smaller hole, and it was possible to live, though, we should think, hard to breathe, in the chamber. Very soon beads of persperation shone in the firelight on the dark, copper-coloured skin, and the chant grew louder as the heat entered the old man's bones. The moisture streamed off him as the red embers glowed, and still his song went on, like no other we had ever listened to, wavering and quavering, but continuous.

We stood and watched him for ten minutes or so, while the evening light faded away from the sky, and the white mist rose in wreaths over the grass and clover fields. Presently the old fellow rose from his shelf and struggled out of his hole and marched off as he was, down the road for a couple of hundred yards, and then popped into a deep hole in the river and sat there for a few seconds. Then he got out, shook himself, passed his hands over his limbs, and proceeded to put on his clothes.

Wallis Nash, on observing an "old Coquelle chief" taking a sweat-bath on the Siletz Reserve in 1877

overleaf
Heceta Head: the Lighthouse

Dunes near Honeyman Park

Moss hangs from tree near Oswald West State Park

You are a great chief, so am I. This is my country. I was here when these trees were very small, not higher than my head. My heart is sick with fighting but I want to live in my country. If the white men are willing I will go back to Deer Creek and live among them as I used to; they can visit my camp and I will visit theirs but I will not lay down my arms and go to the reservation, I will fight.

Chief John to Lieutenant Robert C. Buchanan, May 26, 1856. The Chief, leader of the Ech-ka-tw-a clan of Josephine County refused to be moved to the Grande Ronde Reservation in Yamhill County. Fierce fighting ensued. Even in defeat, Chief John continued to struggle, leading eventually to his imprisonment at Alcatraz. Certainly both the words and actions of this great Oregon warrior bely the notion that coastal Natives were placid, easily subdued peoples.

Back 460 years — legend says in 1492 — an old Chinaman survived the wreck of his junk on the Oregon shore to turn pirate with a cut-throat band of redskins:

From broad Columbia down to Coos
they fiercely swooped in great canoes
To Orford, Coos and far Coquille
they hewed away with gleaming steel.

Emil Peterson and Alfred Pavers, from *A Century of Coos and Curry*

Detail, driftwood and sand

Beach at early morning, north of Cape Kiwanda

View north from Cape Lookout

Looking north towards Cape Kiwanda's Rock Beehive

You are hereby instructed that if you make any fort or improvement on the coast, be sure you purchase the soil from the natives. Let the instrument of conveyance bear every authentic mark the circumstances will permit. We cannot forbear to impress on your mind our will and expectation that the most inviolable harmony and friendship may subsist between you and the natives and that no advantage be taken of them in trading, but that you may endeavor by honest conduct to impress on their minds, friendship for Americans. The sea letters from Congress and from this state you will show on every proper occasion and although we expect you will treat all natives with respect and civility, yet we depend you will suffer insult and injury from none, without showing that spirit which becomes a freeborn and independent American.

Instructions given to Captains Kendrick and Gray before their departure for the Pacific Northwest in the *Columbia* and the *Lady Washington*, in 1787

Wet shrubbery seen through an empty pane in an abandoned house on the southern coast

Because nothing can be done about the rain except blaming. And if nothing can be done about it, why get yourself in a sweat about it? Matter of fact, it can be convenient to have around. Got troubles with the old lady? It's the rain. Got worries and frets about the way the old bus is falling to pieces right under you? It's the ruttin' rain.

Ken Kesey, from *Sometimes a Great Notion*

Lily pad in small lake near southern shoreline

. . . *ubiquitous, continuous, monotonous, formless.*

Bernard Malamud, on the properties of Oregon's coastal rainfall

A young Common murre, the "penguin" of the northern hemisphere

Herring gulls

"That reminds me," he observed. *"Swiveltongue Saunders did say something about a fellow being turned into a gull when he died. Do I have to be a gull? You can't do much with a girl when you're a gull."*

Albert Richard Wetjen, from *Fiddler's Green*

"Painted" rock, Hug Point

Detail, rocks just below Heceta Head

Homes huddled above creek south of Cannon Beach

Empty, every window shattered, an Astoria building recalls with grim irony the man whose ambitions and dreams have become synonomous with the American commercialization and colonization of the Oregon Territory

On the waters of the Pacific we can found no claim in right of Louisiana. If we claim that country at all, it must be on Astor's settlement near the mouth of the Columbia.

Thomas Jefferson

Abandoned house, southern coast

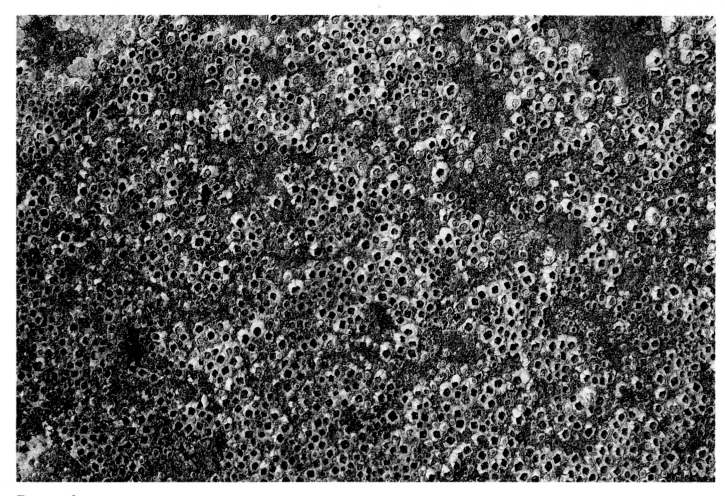

Barnacles

That he sang to me in the moonlight on Panmanok's gray beach,
With the thousand responsive songs at random,
My own songs awakened from that hour,
And with them the key, the word up from the waves,
The word of the sweetest song and all songs,
That strong and delicious word which, creeping to my feet,
(Or like some old crone rocking the cradle, swathed in
sweet garments, bending aside),
The sea whisper'd me.

Walt Whitman, from *Sea Drift*

Coast Range, mist and dunes near Florence

Nothing but vile stinking fogge.

Sir Francis Drake on the meteorological glories of the Cape Arago area, June, 1579

Ocean scene near Port Orford

In this situation the northernmost extremity of the land is formed by a low land projecting from the high rocky coast a considerable way into the sea, and terminating in a wedgelike low perpendicular cliff . . . This I distinguished by the name of Cape Orford, in honour of my much respected friend the noble Earl (George) of that title: off it lies several rocky islets.

Captain George Vancouver, April 24, 1792

Sunset at Haystack Rock, near Cannon Beach

Detail, cedar bark

Fence against wall. Wood against wood. Time, dampness and salt against them all

Sand-scrubbed rocks nestled in hollow of driftwood log

Wind and sand-blasted, faded wood; behind a scratched pane, calm, colors, a stubborn unwillingness to break, bending all the while

S' doaks was son of Yelth the wise —
Chief of the Raven clan.
Itswoot the Bear had him in care
To make him a medicine man.

He was quick and quicker to learn —
Bold and bolder to dare:
He danced the dread Kloo-Kwallie Dance
To tickle Itswoot the Bear!

Oregon Legend

Rudyard Kipling, from *Kim*

Heceta Head

The coast of Oregon faces the longest unimpeded stretch of open ocean on earth — without islands or reefs to buffer the impact of waves born in the seas off Japan, 6,000 miles away.

Mark Miller

Seal Rocks at sunset

Indian ownership of the coast reaches back doubtless for a hundred generations, and a map in 500 A.D. probably would have shown the same ownership as that made by Lewis and Clark 1300 years later.

John P. Harrington, ethnologist

Detail, young fernhead

Detail, fern shadow on leaf

Like an inn from the pages of a Hardy novel, a house near Cannon Beach braces itself for an impending storm

The merchants of Boston felt a peculiar interest in the Oregon country — not only on account of the profit to be derived from the trade in sea otter skins, seal skins and other pelts, but for the further reason that they had always felt that this country belonged to the Commonwealth of Massachusetts. The King of England in 1620, had granted to the Council of Plymouth, the land lying between the 40th and 48th degrees of north latitude, extending from the Atlantic Ocean to the Western Sea. By the terms of this royal grant, Massachusetts owned the Pacific seacoast from Cape Mendocino in California to the Strait of Juan de Fuca, between Vancouver Island and the state of Washington, to say nothing of all the land lying between the Atlantic seaboard and the Pacific Ocean.

Fred Lockley, from *Oregon Trail Blazers*

To all Emperors, Kings, Sovereign Princes, State and Regents, to their respective officers, civil and military, and to all others whom it may concern: I, George Washington, President of the United States of America, do make known that Robert Gray, captain of the ship called the Columbia, of the burthen of about 230 tons, is a citizen of the United States and that the said ship which he commands, belongs to citizens of the United States and as I wish that the said Robert Gray may prosper in his lawful affairs, I do request of all the aforementioned and of each of them separately, when the said Robert Gray shall arrive with his vessel and cargo they will be pleased to receive him with kindness and treat him in a becoming manner and thereby I shall consider myself obliged.

September 16, 1799, George Washington, President; Thomas Jefferson, Secretary of State, signed with the Seal of the United States.

Looking south from Hug Point

Fresh water channel heads for the sea on southern coast

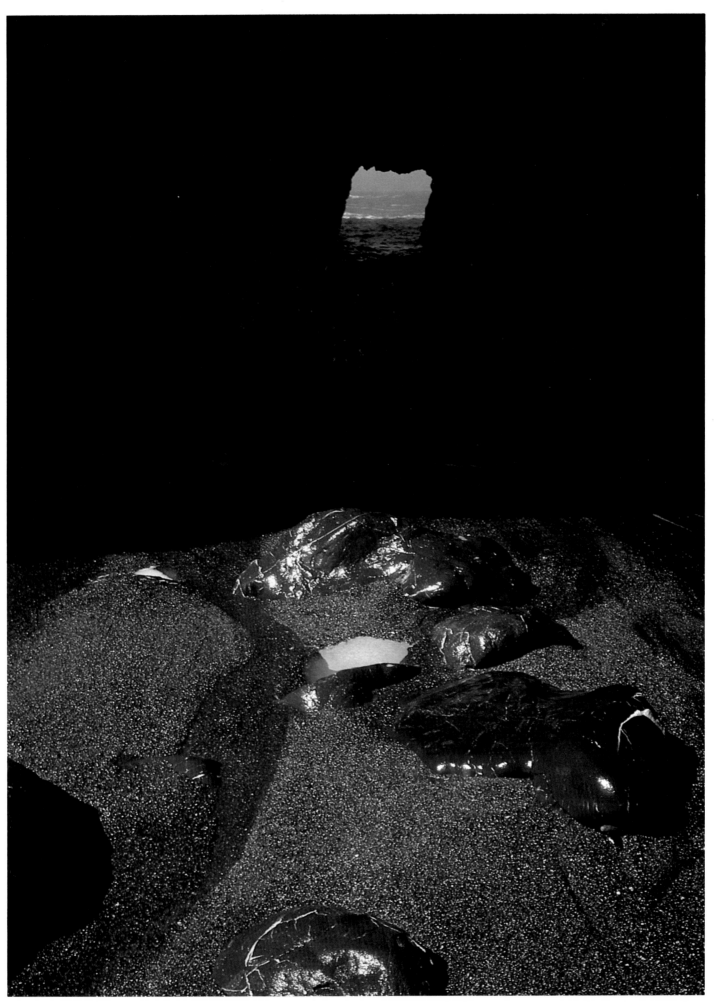

Cave shaped like an Oregon map under Sister Rocks, southern coast

Detail, NOMA house near Hammond at the mouth of the Columbia River

Shore birds and surf, Cape Kiwanda

. . . Slaves to the waves: pause too long pecking out a morsel from the running sand and WATCH OUT all the others turn *run run back except one careless bird, and when the wave rolls back a gray-speckled dot kicks desperately to free its wing from the sand before the next wave run run run turn run run run back . . .*

Ken Kesey, from *Sometimes a Great Notion*

Skunk Cabbage in a coastal forest after an early morning shower.

Colony of White pelicans

Sister Rocks, southern coast

"Ah! The good old time. Youth and the sea. Glamour and the sea! The good, strong sea, the salt, bitter sea, that could whisper to you and knock your breath out of you."

Joseph Conrad, from *Typhoon and Other Tales of the Sea*

Crashing surf at Devil's Churn

Near the mouth of the Rogue River, in the vicinity of Gold Beach

The Coast Range, early morning

Why . . . those Indians down the coast, combined with their brothers, the Rough River Indians, are the worst Indians on the American continent, and the bravest. Every old settler in Oregon knows that.

Jesse Applegate

Beach, after a storm

A classic view of Oregon coastline seen from Cape Lookout, looking south

Night view south from Ecola State Park, south of Tillamook Head

The seashore is a sort of neutral ground, a most advantageous point from which to contemplate this world. It is even a trivial place. The waves forever rolling to the land are too far-travelled and untamable to be familiar. Creeping along the endless beach amid the sun-squawl and the foam, it occurs to us that we, too, are the product of sea slime.

It is a wild, rank place, and there is no flattery in it. Strewn with crabs, horse-shoes, and razor-clams, and whatever the sea casts up — a vast morgue, *where the carcasses of men and beasts together lie stately upon its shelf, rotting and bleaching in the sun and waves, and each tide turns them in their beds, and tucks fresh sand under them. There is naked Nature — inhumanly sincere, wasting no thought on man, nibbling at the cliffy shore where gulls wheel amid the spray.*

Henry David Thoreau, 1883

White-crowned sparrow

He had stripped, to a pair of clean white drawers, and wore a scarlet waistband. A plume of white and magenta feathers rose high from a bead head-dress, and another plume was bound on each arm, and he carried a plume in each hand. The black bands and vermillion patches on his face were freshly touched up.

The women had black stiff petticoats, and scarlet capes round their shoulders, with rows upon rows of large blue and white necklaces hung round their necks. They also carried feathers in their hands.

Chief Kaseeah, of the Alceas, and family, posing for a portrait at their beach camp near Yaquina Bay, described by Wallis Nash in 1878

A Ticket machine in an empty amusement arcade, Seaside. Even these symbols of tawdry early-fifties commercialism have begun to subtly change; their harsh edges sanded down, their colors, while still bright, fading like a rainbow seen through a light mist. They, too, have become a part of this coast.

Rocks on beach near Heceta Head

overleaf
Abandoned dance hall, Pacific City

Detail, driftwood and stone on beach

You can almost see the Indian canoes on the ocean in the rain.

Ken Kesey

Bluff and storm near Oswald West State Park

The storm was gradually increasing and the roaring of the surf and the shaking of the island was calculated to disturb weak nerves. The clouds were flying overhead like frightened gulls and occasional gusts brought snow and rain. The surf was thrown completely over the island and even dashed against the lenses of the light almost 100 feet above the low tide.

Chandler B. Watson, describing the situation facing rescuers preparing to go to the aid of the stricken steam collier *Tacoma* above the mouth of the Umpqua in 1883

Great blue herons flocking over shoals of fish at low tide near Cape Lookout

Ocean near Boiler Bay

. . . that on the seventh, desirous of reaching the ship agreeably to their promise, they had quitted Chinook point, in spite of the remonstrances of the chief, Concomly, who sought to detain them by pointing out the danger to which they would expose themselves in crossing the bay in such heavy sea as it was; that they had scarcely made more than a mile and a half before a huge wave broke over their boat and capsized it; that the Indians, aware of the danger to which they were exposed, had followed them, and that, but for their assistance, Mr. M'Dougal, who could not swim, would inevitably have been drowned; that, after the Chinooks had kindled a large fire and dried their clothes, they had been conducted by them back to their village, where the principal chief had received them with all imaginable hospitality, regaling them with every delicacy his wigwam afforded; that, in fine, if they had got back safe and sound to the vessel, it was to the timely succor and humane cares of the Indians whom we saw before us that they owed it. We liberally rewarded these generous children of the forest, and they returned home well satisfied.

Gabriel Franchere, from *Narrative of a Voyage to the Northwest Coast of America*

Looking south from Cape Meares

The sea remembers nothing. It is feline. It licks your feet — its huge flanks purr very pleasantly for you; but it will crack your bones and eat you, for all that, and wipe the crimsoned foam from its jaws as if nothing had happened. The mountains give their lost children berries and water; the sea mocks their thirst and lets them die. The mountains have a grand, stupid, loveable tranquility; the sea has a fascinating, treacherous intelligence. The mountains lie about like huge ruminants, their broad backs awful to look upon, but safe to handle. The sea smooths its silver scales, until you cannot see their joints . . . The mountains dwarf mankind and fore-shorten the procession of its long generations. The sea drowns out humanity and time; it has no sympathy with either; for it belongs to eternity, and of that it sings its monotonous song forever and ever.

Oliver Wendell Holmes, from *The Autocrat of the Breakfast Table*

overleaf

Sunset, Cape Blanco, westernmost point of the forty-eight adjacent states

For all that has been said of the love that certain natures (on shore) have professed to feel for it, for all the celebrations it has been the object of in prose and song, the sea has never been friendly to man. At most it has been the accomplice of human restlessness.

Joseph Conrad, from *The Mirror of the Sea*

OREGON/THE COAST

Production Information

Design	Randy Morse and John A. Wood
Editing	Randy Morse
Production Coordination	Reidmore Pocol Enterprises Ltd.
Artwork	Alice Hjort
Press Supervisor	Ernest Schermann
Printing	Stuart Brandle Printing Services Ltd.
Separations	Color Graphics Ltd. The original color photographs were separated on a Hell DC-300B Laser scanner, which electronically screened the transparencies at 200 lines per inch
Endsheets	Tweedweave
Jackets	60 lb. varnished Centura Gloss Cover
Typeface	16/16 Schoolbook
Paper	100 lb. Imperial Gloss
Publisher	Reidmore Books Oregon Inc. 4851 Donald Street Eugene, Oregon 97405 U.S.A.

Printed and bound in Canada

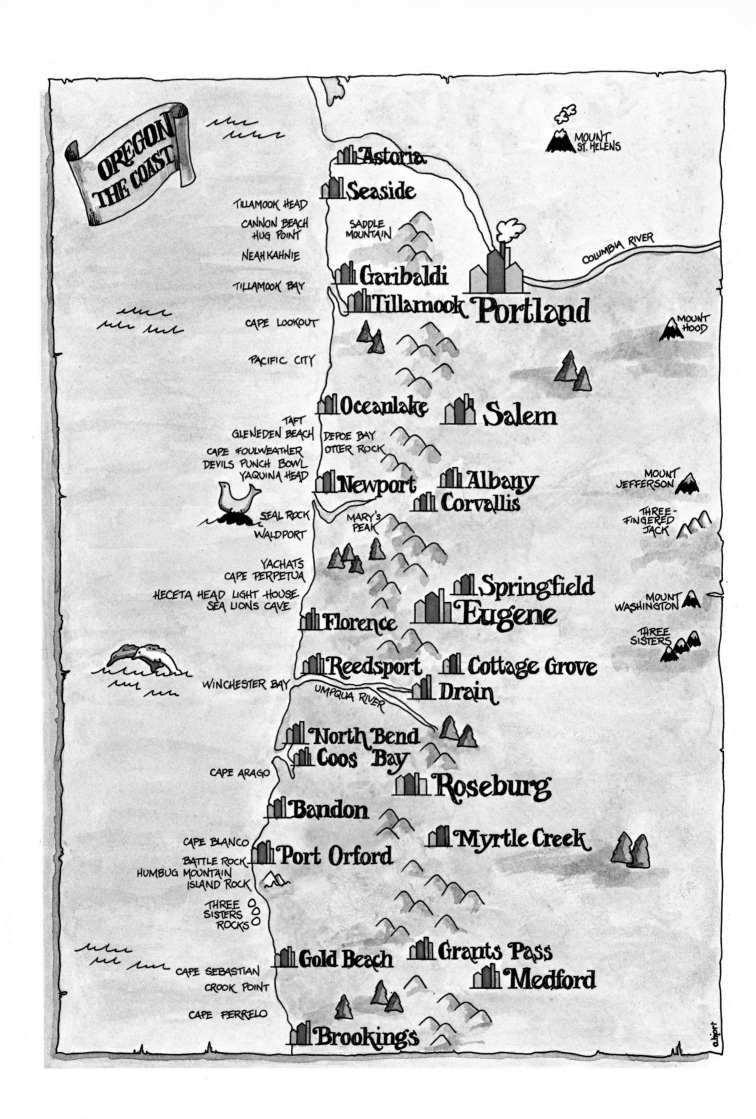